# NATTER

## BACHEM Ba 349

## and other German rocket fighter projects

Joachim Dressel

**Schiffer Military/Aviation History**
Atglen, PA

## Sources
- Archives of the Heinkel concern
- Collection of the German Museum, Munich
- Archives of the Research Group for Aviation History
- Compiler's archives
- Collection of M. Griehl
- Collection of M. Emmerling

## Picture Credits
- M. Boehme
- German Museum, Munich
- M. Emmerling
- M. Griehl
- M. Hensel
- R. Lutz
- J. Meier
- F. Mueller-Romminger
- W. Radinger
- F. Selinger
- G. Sengfelder
- H. Stapfer
- F. Trenkle
- R. Zobel

Printed in the United States of America
ISBN: 0-88740-682-3

This title was originally published under the title, *Natter Bachem Ba 349; und andere deutsche Kleinsraketenjäger,* by Podzun-Pallase Verlag.

We are interested in hearing from authors with book ideas on related topics.

A model of the Heinkel He 176. This was the premier aircraft for manned rocket flight. The aircraft was built in 1938.

Translated from the German by Curtis Bond

Published by Schiffer Publishing Ltd.
77 Lower Valley Road
Atglen, PA 19310
Please write for a free catalog.
This book may be purchased from the publisher.
Please include $2.95 postage.
Try your bookstore first.

# THE SMALL ROCKET FIGHTER

In the course of the Second World War, the over-whelming force of the Allies was shown again and again. The leadership of the Luftwaffe therefore looked into the possibility of producing inexpensive aircraft which, however, would have enough power to quickly engage the enemy formations. Consequently, the machines which were created were predominately made of wood, a raw material not important to the war effort. Assembly and construction were kept as simple as possible. In this way these machines could be completed without affecting the already overloaded industry. The rocket motor was a natural choice for a power plant due to its high performance. The take-off and landing procedures were kept simple to avoid long training periods for pilots. Take-off was accomplished via a tow or a vertical take-off. Landing was made on skids or the fighter was abandoned and the pilot and important components (e.g. motor, weapons systems) recovered by parachute.

What follows is the history of the development of these technically highly-interesting aircraft. Unfortunately, no photos exist from most of these projects, many do not even have existing drawings.

Right:
The Arado Ar 234 C-3 was to carry the rocket fighter project Ar E381 to altitude.

## ARADO E381

This small fighter was created presumably in the fall of 1944 as a project in which a rocket-powered, heavily-armored fighter sporting a MK 108 cannon would be carried under an Ar 234 C-3 to the enemy formation. Its weight was 1,200 kilos. The pilot lay prone in the cockpit behind 140mm of armored glass and was protected by 27mm-thick armored plate. The squat design had the following dimensions:

Length: 4.95m; Height: 1.20m; Wingspan; 5.0m; Wing Area 5.0sqm.

The fighter was to have been taken to 6000m within eight minutes by the Ar 234. After separation the pilot would go into a steep dive, switch on the HWK 109-509 B engine and reach 900km/h in a few seconds. Once in the target area, the machine had a combat radius of approximately 30km. The remaining range of 120km was needed for the return flight to a suitable landing field. The landing was made on skids. After dismantling the machine into approximately twelve pieces, the aircraft could be taken back to its home airfield in an ordinary lorry.

Because of the drawback that the pilot could not get out of the aircraft once it was hung under the Ar 234, a new cockpit was developed with a side entrance. The height was reduced by 0.7m, and the fuselage length grew to 5.70m. The wing tips were bend downward. A rocket motor with a cruise burner was used. Instead of a MK 108, RZ 73 spin-stabilized rockets were proposed. Neither project materialized.

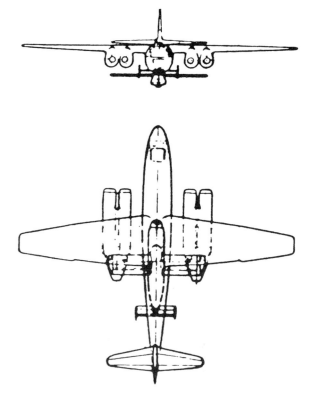

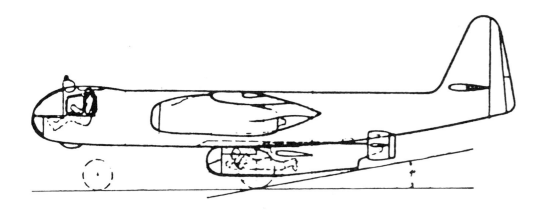

8-234 C3 mit Kleinstjäger E-381

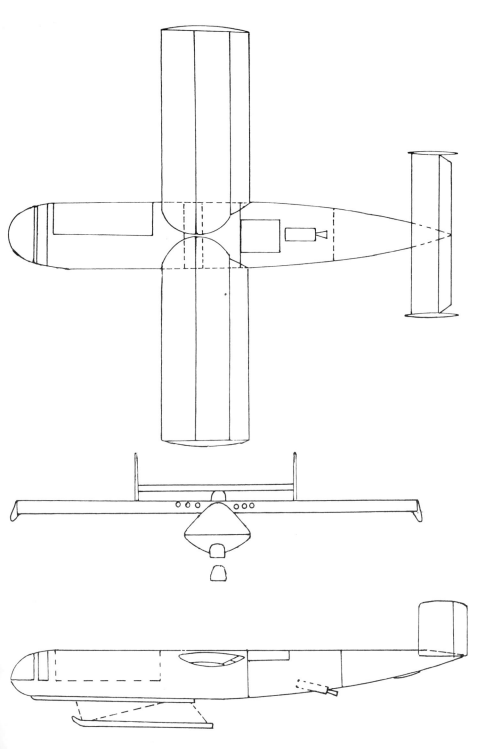

Above: Small manned rocket fighter Arado Ar E 381 in front of an Arado Ar 234 C-3.

Left:
Drawing of the second design of the Arado Ar E 381 with side entrance.

Below:
Model of the Ar E 381.

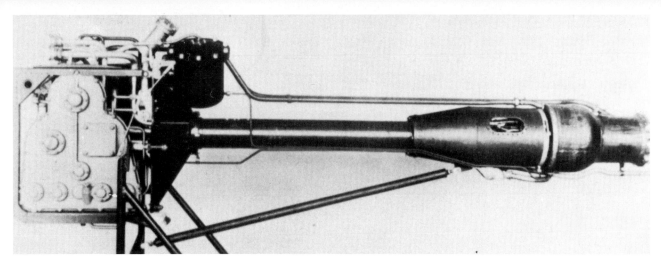

Left:
Left side view of the HWK 109-509 A without afterburner.

Below:
Drawing of the Walter Rocket Motor HWK 109-509 C with cruise burners. The Walter engine was used as propulsion for most of the rocket fighter projects because it was the most advanced machine available.

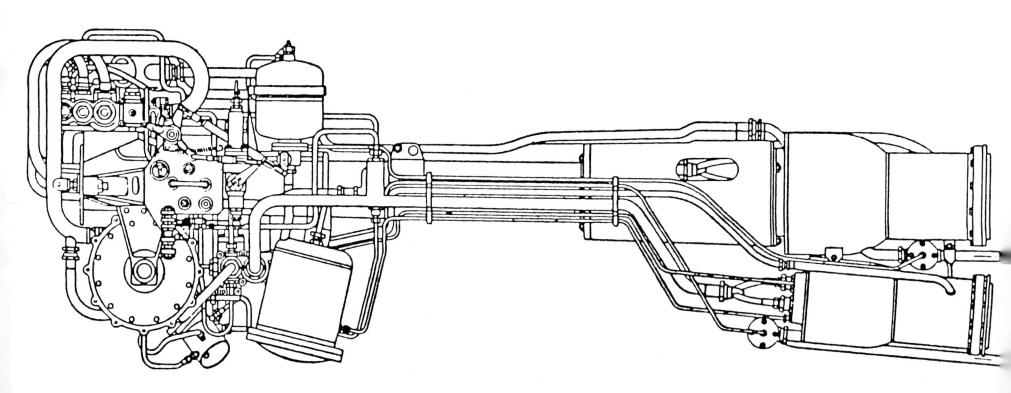

Right:
Total view of the HWK 109-509 A, as it was also
used in the Me 163.

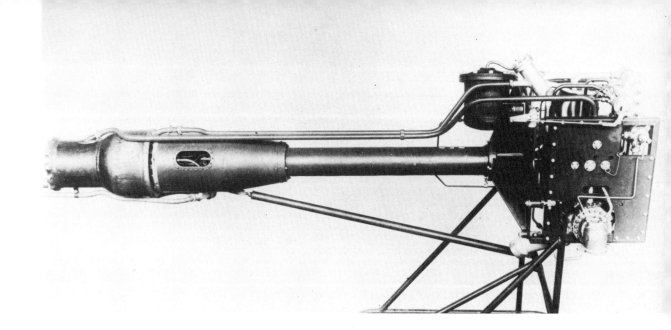

Below:
Detail photos looking aft of the HWK 109-509 A.

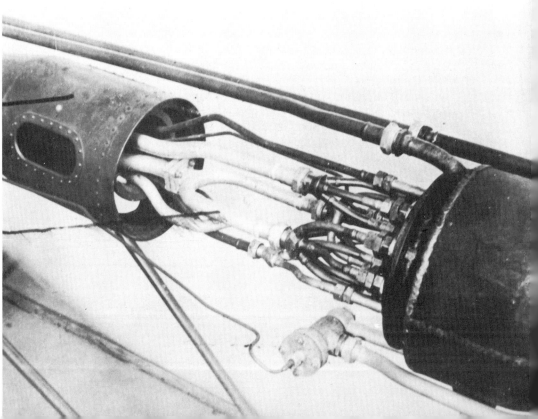

# DFS "EBER"

Institute A of the German Research Institute for Gliding Flight (DFS) in Ainring developed the "Eber" as a general purpose machine. The aircraft was towed by a pole to a position above the enemy formation behind a Fw 190 or Me 262. After the first attack the pilot could switch on rocket motors and complete a second pass. The pilot then had to disengage from the battle and eject from the aircraft. This was accomplished by a parachute pulling the pilot and his seat from the cockpit. After slowing his decent from 40m/s to 25-30m/s the pilot separated from the seat. The fighter would be written off as a total loss. This system meant no recovery of the aircraft was necessary. Pilot training concentrated only on the attack phase; the complicated matters of take off and landing procedures could be eliminated.

In addition to the possibility of shooting down an enemy bomber, there was also the possibility of ramming. The disposable machine would be flown directly at the enemy plane. The pilot was protected by armor plating. The problem was the immense deceleration forces of up to 400g which would arise. The human body can normally only withstand 15g. With padding these high g-forces could be reduced, however, where was there room for it in a small fighter?

# Zeppelin "Rammer"

This project was originally conceived to ram enemy aircraft (including fighters). The 5.1m long, 1.7m high, and 4.9m wide "Rammer" had a take-off weight of only 860kg. Both 1000kp producing Schmidding 109-533 solid fuel rocket engines would be fastened to the four tubular spars of the wings and would also serve to stiffen the fuselage. The pilot was encased in an cockpit with up to 30mm of armor plating. The armored windscreen was 90mm thick. A production contract was let in November 1944 to the IG Farben concern.

Take-off was accomplished on a tricycle carriage, the landing on skids.

# "Flying Panzerfaust"

This project also presumably came from the Zeppelin works. It dealt with an aircraft filled with high explosives, which the pilot was to use in carrying out a suicide attack on an enemy bomber. Later this idea was scrapped and an ejection system was constructed. The 6.0m-long machine had a span of 4.5m, however, a wing area of 3.8sqm led to a wing loading of 320 kg/sqm. The six solid fuel rockets, three on each side of the fuselage behind the wings, propelled the fighter to 850km/h. Neither project materialized.

Here and overleaf:
Original model of the So 344 from 1944. Clearly recognizable are the detachable armored nose with the four stabilizing fins and the two machine guns for the second attack.

## SOMBOLD SO 344

In January 1944, the Bley engineering office from Naumburg/Saale submitted the plans for a "ramming fighter" (Rammschussjaeger). The idea was to attach a 400kg warhead to the front of a very simply built aircraft. The warhead would be jettisoned into the midst of the enemy formation where it would explode. This would totally disrupt the bomber group. The aircraft itself could then make additional attacks by using its two machine guns. Take off was accomplished in tow and the landing on skids. The So 344 was to have been 7.0m long, 2.18m high, have a 5.7m wingspan, and a take-off weight of 1350kg. Neither this nor the two following designs from Messerschmitt were put into production.

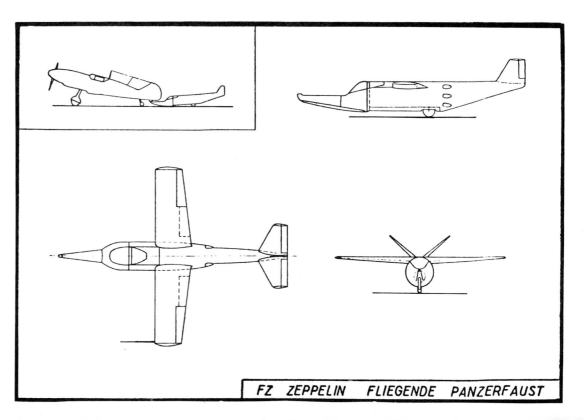

FZ ZEPPELIN FLIEGENDE PANZERFAUST

## Messerschmitt ME P.1103

This design from the summer of 1944 represented a ramming fighter with a heavily armored nose and up to six armored windows. The pilot steered from a prone position within a 10mm thick armored cylinder which had a steel plate door. Behind this cylinder was a wooden empennage which was derived from the V1 project.

Like other ramming fighters, after attacking, the pilot was to disengage from the battle and be pulled from the fighter with his seat by a parachute. The armored cell would descend under a large recovery parachute. This would allow the cockpit with its four floor-mounted RI-202 engines and two MK 108 machine guns to be used again. Under the 79cm-tall fuselage was a rearward firing 21cm rocket launcher as defensive armament. The machine had a length of 4.7m, a wing area of 5.8sqm, and weighed 1110kg. A planned second variant of the P.1103, a shipboard fighter (Bordjaeger), had the pilot sitting upright, without armor, and a single MK 108.

## Messerschmitt P.1104

A design from 22 September 1944 shows the towed fighter with a shoulder-mounted wing, a span of 6.2m, and a HWK-109-509-A-1 rocket engine. Here too, the pilot sat in an armored box. The ramming attack was to be followed by a strafing attack using the MK 108 with 30mm high explosive shells. The 800km/h, 2540kg machine was to have a range of 90km, a maximum altitude of 13000m and land on skids.

A variation of this project which was considered was a midwing monoplane with smaller dimensions. This design had the temporary designation S 53.

All of these studies were relegated to the archives as the leaders of the Luftwaffe and the fighter staff discarded the idea of a small fighter and decided on the conventional Me 262 A-1 and the He 162 A-1/A-2 (Volksjaeger).

Mock-ups and prototypes were built of the Heinkel "Julia", the Junkers "Wally", and the Bachem "Natter" which will be described now.

Below:
The goal of all the designers was the development of a weapon to break the massive allied air attacks.

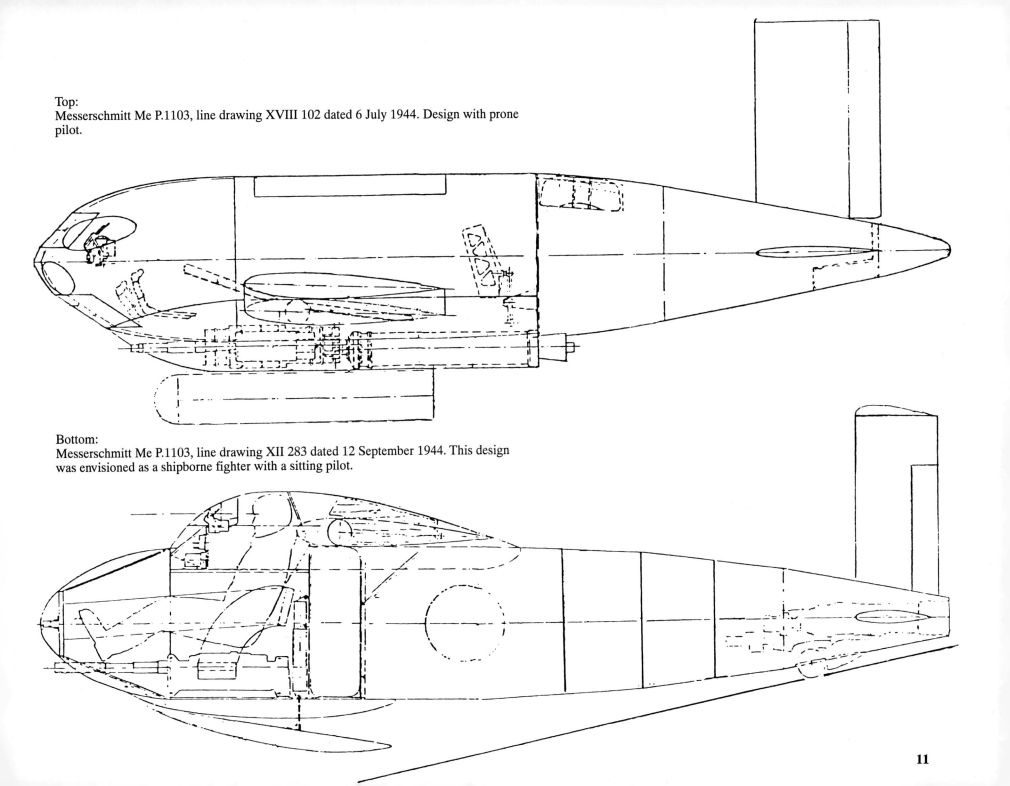

Top:
Messerschmitt Me P.1103, line drawing XVIII 102 dated 6 July 1944. Design with prone pilot.

Bottom:
Messerschmitt Me P.1103, line drawing XII 283 dated 12 September 1944. This design was envisioned as a shipborne fighter with a sitting pilot.

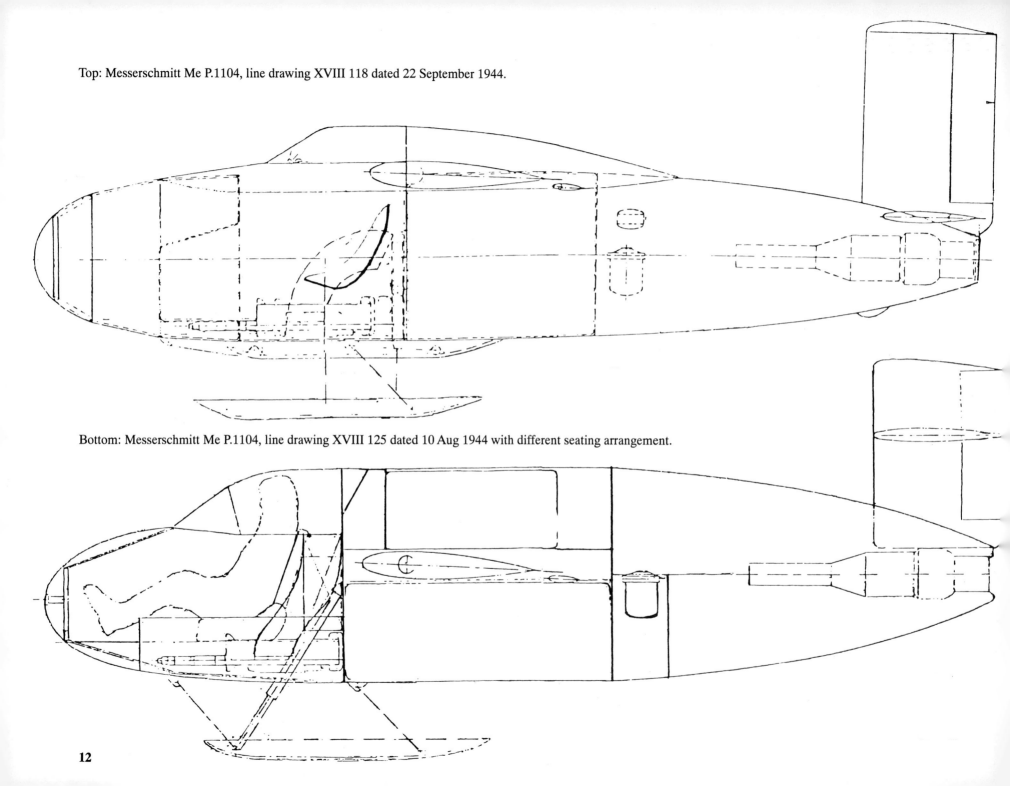

Top: Messerschmitt Me P.1104, line drawing XVIII 118 dated 22 September 1944.

Bottom: Messerschmitt Me P.1104, line drawing XVIII 125 dated 10 Aug 1944 with different seating arrangement.

## Heinkel P.1077 "Julia"

In the early summer of 1944, W. Benz and Dr. Gerloff began to finalize the first sketches of Project 1068, a rocket fighter of simplistic construction. Documents of the EHAG dated 19 August 1944 show a small shoulder wing aircraft with an almost circular fuselage and twin vertical stabilisers. Propulsion would come from a HWK with climb/cruise burners and two booster rockets on either side of the fuselage. Armament consisted of two specially constructed MG 151/20. The wooden craft, codenamed "Julia", was 6.98m long, had a wingspan of 4.6m and was 2.00m tall. The fuselage was 0.95m wide.

As early as 8 September 1994, the State Ministry of Aviation (RLM) let a contract for the construction of 20 prototype aircraft. Director Franke from Heinkel assumed overall planning and transferred the construction of the prototypes to the Vienna woodworks which had sufficient expansion room and equipment. Construction required two men each for the wings and the fuselage as well as two propulsion specialists, a flight control specialist, a specialist for the fuel system, and four designers from Heinkel. The construction of the prototypes required a master woodworker, the 25 aircraft carpenters and two experienced fitters from the Vienna woodworks. The engineer Ludwig Hoffman was lead test pilot for Bachem and Heinkel, theoretical work was supported by Professor Schrenk as well as Dipl. Ing. Küttner from TH Vienna. The overall leadership was entrusted, as before, to W. Benz. The "Julia" was to be constructed on normal workbenches as a simple carpentry project.

14 days later, orders were given to build 300 complete machines per month. At the same time "Julia" received the project number 1077. The previous number, P.1068, went to the He P.343, a four-engined jet bomber project. On 15 October 1944, the RLM was offered more plans of the utility aircraft. For example, a version with four solid fuel rockets attached to the sides of the fuselage and a Walter engine. The armament was changed from four pod-mounted MG 151/20 to MK 108's in the fuselage. Another variant was proposed with two skids and a sitting pilot. Additionally, a simplified version of the "Julia" was displayed. With this, the rocket engine was replaced by a pulse jet. The codename for this was "Romeo."

On the 26th of October 1944, Professor Heinkel and his construction staff decided on the version with a prone pilot. The fuselage was unchanged, the wings retained their rectangular form for ease of mass production. Enlarging the profile in order to increase the engine size was discussed. The flaps would also serve as rudders. The twin vertical stabilizer was abandoned in favour of a single one. Armament consisted of two MK 108's sitting on both sides of the pilot.

Below: A post-war drawing of the "Julia."

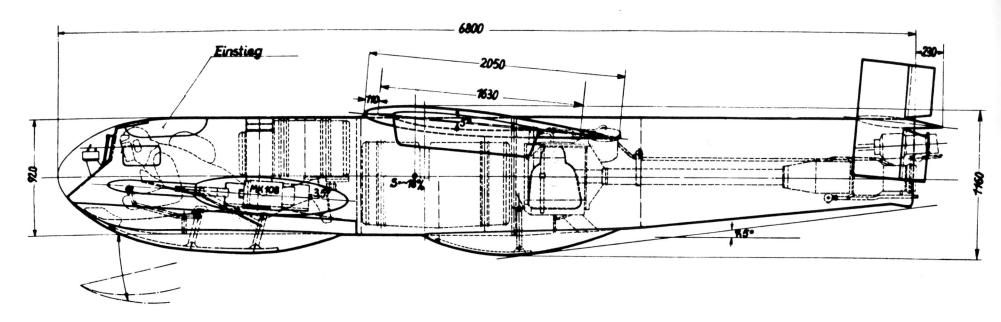

Top: Plans of the "Julia" with prone pilot. The drawing was made after the war from original documents.

Bottom: This drawing shows the second version of the "Julia" with sitting pilot. These plans were created from documents from Heinkel dated September 1944.

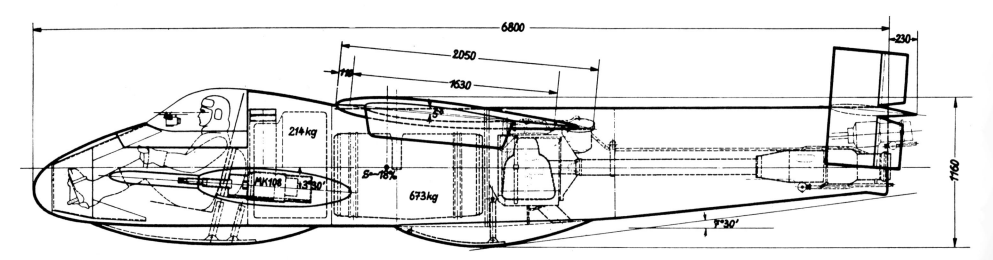

Completion of individual pieces for the rocket fighter "Julia" by Heinkel in the Vienna woodworks at the end of 1944. After the bombardment of the workshops, production was moved to Krems.

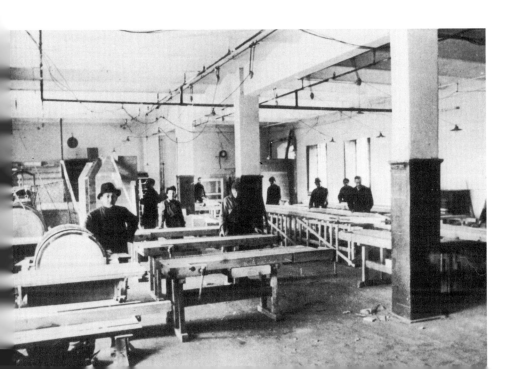

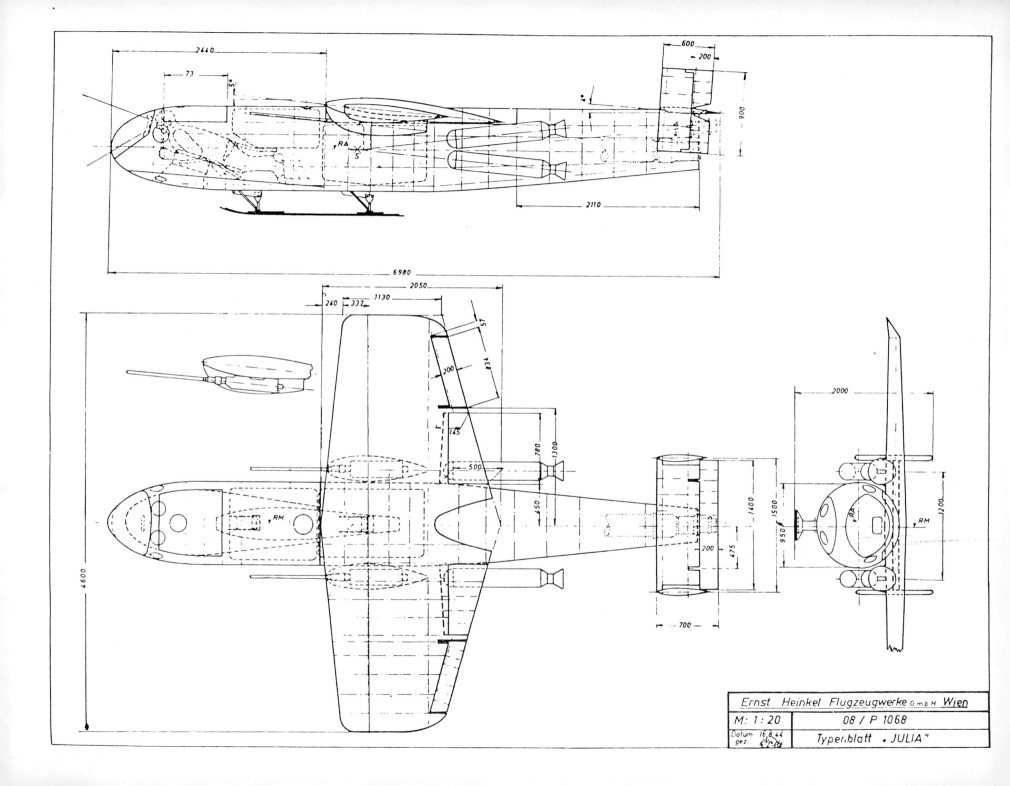

| Ernst Heinkel Flugzeugwerke GmbH Wien | |
|---|---|
| M: 1:20 | 08 / P 1068 |
| Datum 16.8.44 gez. | Typenblatt „JULIA" |

Instrumentation proved to be spartan: Altimeter, airspeed and pitch indicators, compass, stop watch, and engine controls.

Take-off was to be made vertically and landing made on skids. This was the difference in tactical employment of the "Julia" and its competition, the Bachem "Natter."

In October 1944, work was begun on a 1/20 scale flight model. Meanwhile, director Luscher suggested production of the P.1077 with sitting pilot, modified empennage, and thicker, rectangular wings with a smaller span. There was no compromising between Benz and Luscher and it was decided to produce both versions. Scale models for speed and take off testing were completed by the end of 1944. Different empennage variations could also be tested. Near the Hamburg canal, towing trials were held with a full scale mock-up.

An aerial attack on the Vienna woodworks a short time later destroyed the first full mock-up, plans, and completed components. A search was launched to find a place to construct the first five prototype aircraft. The lot fell on the Geppert concern in Krems/Donau. Trained personnel were already there because the firm was entrusted with completion of the He 162. Roll out of the first "Julia" was to take place on 15 January 1945 even though the plans were originally delivered from Heinkel on 13 December 1944. This was an omen of things to come.

During the work the use of a different skid arrangement as well as the inclusion of an ejection seat was to be finalized. Geppert suggested lengthening the fuselage to allow for a larger fuel tank and extended range. Except for model trials, no decision was forthcoming. Additionally, Geppert could not support the project further because their entire capacity was needed for the construction of the He 162. The Schäfer concern in Linz now assumed responsibility for the construction of the prototypes. They were temporarily to construct only two unpowered and two powered prototypes. Both unpowered prototypes were already 90% completed.

Left:
The Spitzerberg near Hainburg in Austria. Flying tests of models of the "Julia" were conducted here.

Right:
In this hanger of the Spitzerberg flight school, prototypes of the He P.1077 were assembled.

In March 1945 Benz was forced to turn over the direction of prototype construction to Jost. The entire development work on Project 1077 was now concentrated in Neuhaus. By the end of the war, W. Benz maintained, five more test prototypes could be produced, at least one of which should be flown.

The liberation of Neuhaus on the Triesting by Soviet troops in the beginning of April 1945 ended the development of the "Julia."

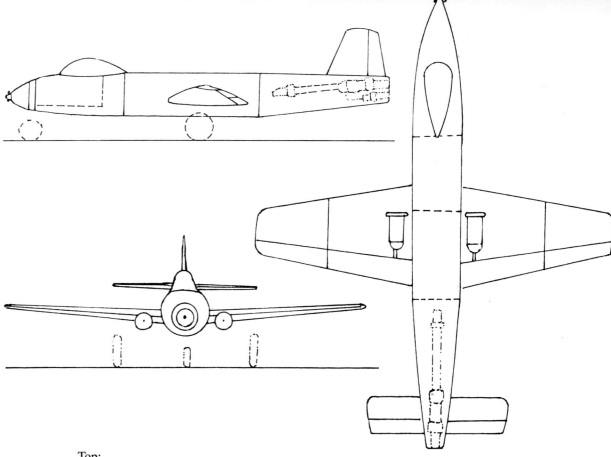

Top:
3-view drawing of the Junkers Ju EF.127 "Wally."

## JUNKERS "WALLY"

Junkers had three developmental aircraft named "Lilly" (an attack aircraft with a pulse jet impulse duct), "Elly" (a bomber), and the fighter and deep penetration aircraft "Wally." The "Wally" was planned with a HWK 105-509 A-1 as well as two 1000kp take-off assist rockets, have a span of 6.65m, a length of 7.80m, and a take-off weight of 2960kg. Take-off and landing were conventional on skids. It was to be possible to climb to 10,000m in 75 seconds. The planners calculated a flight endurance of 11.5 minutes. It was to be armed with two MG 151/20 or two MG 213 and twelve rockets. Arming with conventional bombs was also considered. This was never put into production.

Opposite page:
Left:
Drawings of the "Lilly."
Right top:

Mock-up of the rocket fighter and deep strike aircraft Junkers EF.127 "Wally."

Right bottom:
Wind tunnel model of the Junkers project "Lilly", an attack aircraft with a pulse jet.

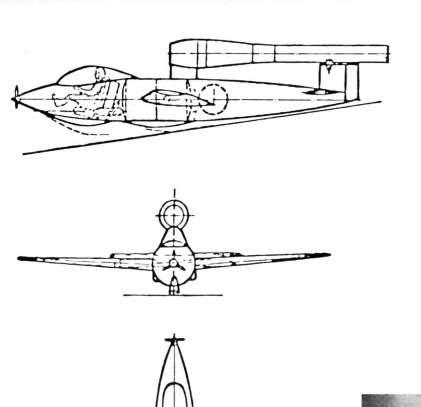
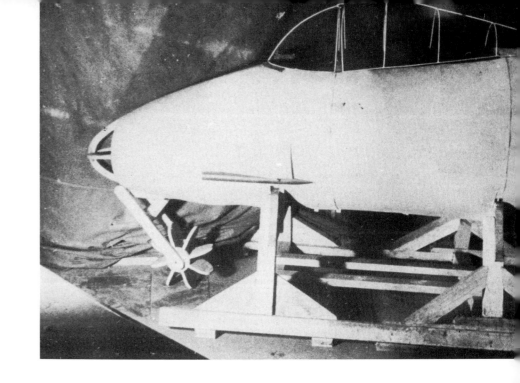
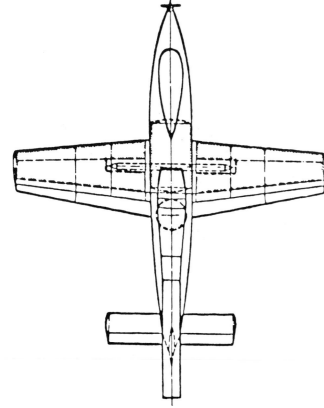
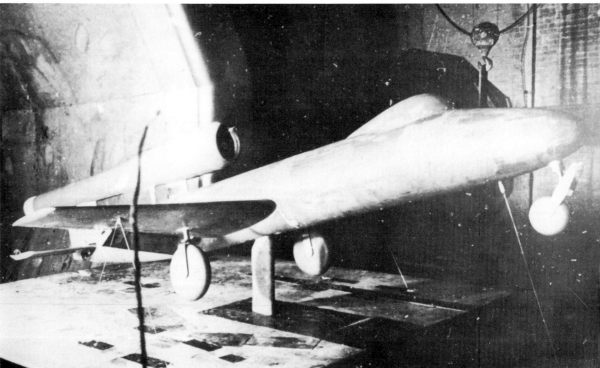

# Bachem Ba 349 "Natter"

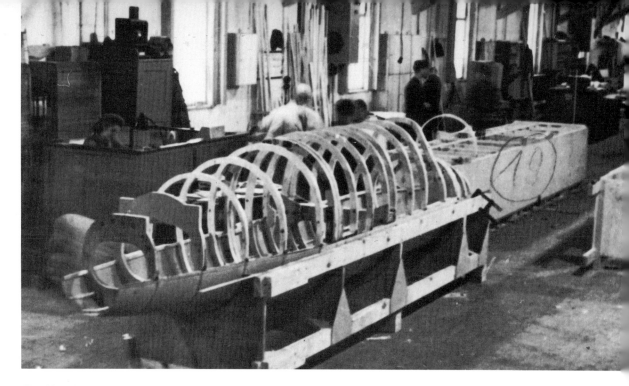

The fast-climbing fighter created in Waldsee/Würtemberg, was presumably heavily influenced after the summer of 1944 by the group surrounding Erich Bachem who was the acting foreman.

Hans Jordanoff, one of Bachem's closed co-workers, persuaded the RLM to be excited about the "Natter."

The OKL-Chief TLR and the SS Main head-quarters were concurrently working on the design.

One of the most important design principles was the use of a launch gantry for vertical take-off. This would enable the aircraft to be used from practically any location, even as a shipboard fighter. The aircraft was powered by a HWK 102-509 A-2 and four solid fuel rockets. Because the danger of an unplanned explosion of the special fuels during landing was always a possibility, Bachem suggested separate parachute landings of pilot and aircraft. This had the added benefit that future "Natter" pilots would only have to be trained in flying and shooting and the long training for take-offs and landings could be discarded. Only the weapon systems and a portion of the cockpit would be lost.

In its original form, the project, called the Bachem BP 20, had a length of 5.72m, a wing-span of 3.20m, a height of 1.17m, and a take-off weight of 1710kg. Armament consisted of two MK 108 and 24 "Föhn" rockets. Later, 48 of these spin-stabilized rockets were used. After reaching its maximum altitude of 12000m, the aircraft would have an average speed of 800km/h and a range of 20km. Because of this, the "Natter" was appropriately nicknamed the "Manned Flak Rocket."

Looking forward at the fuselage of the Bachem Ba 349 "Natter" on a jig. The beams and lower shell are assembled; below, the fuselage spars are already glued.

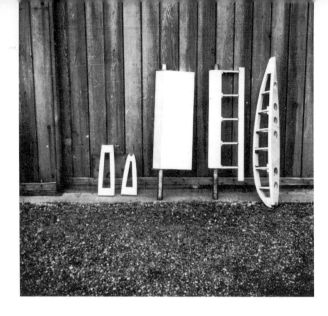

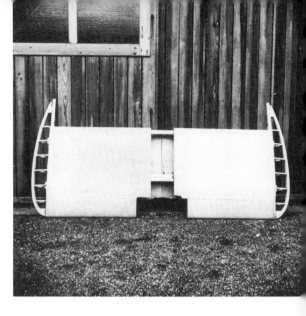

The wings of the "Natter" in various degrees of completion. The wooden construction of the BP-20 had the advantage of avoiding vital war materials and the ease of construction. The wing halves of the Ba 349 could be produced with relatively simple tools.

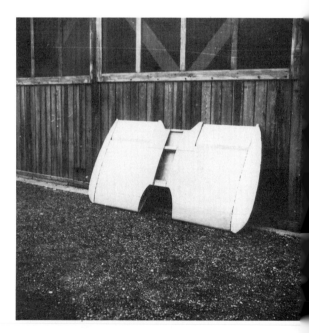

Above: Finished nose sections of the Bachem "Natter."

Above: The fuselage skin was scrap wood and attached to the spans by glue.

Left: The frames for the 60mm-thick armored windscreen was bolted to the nose of the aircraft. The plexiglass side windows were 10mm thick.

In September 1944 an order was placed for 15 Bachem BP-20-prototypes. Additionally, the project was redesignated 8-349 under the emergency fighter program. Full tooling and construction of all components of the BP-20 was begun.

As early as October of the same year, Bachem issued a completion certificate for the "Natter" based on the development documents and the test machines BP 20 M1 and M2 which were already under construction. (Starting at the end of 1944, the designation "M" replaced "V" which stood for test prototype.)

Essentially, the RLM believed the Bachem design was an effective defensive weapon to use against four-engined bombers such as the B-17 or the B-24. As well as increasing production of flak rockets, an order dated 04 November 1944 directed the investigation and construction of "other special weapons", which included the Bachem Ba 349.

In December 1944 came the completion of the prototypes M1, with take-off carriage, as well as the M2 and M3 with fixed undercarriages which had been taken from a Klemm Kl 35. It is uncertain if the M2 ever flew or if it was used solely as a stationary mock-up.

The first step in the direction of a powered "Natter" followed with the acquisition on 3 December 1944 of a 109-509 A-1 from the Walter factory in Beerberg in Schlesien nach Waldsee. A take-off attempt with this engine was, however, postponed.

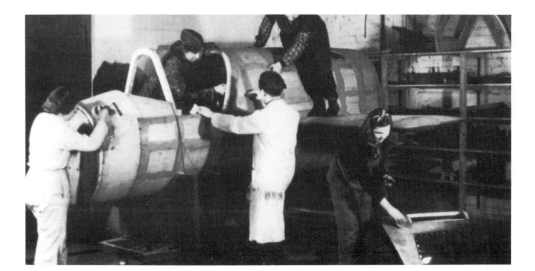

Above: Fuselage completion of a BP-20. Women were used more and more as the war progressed.

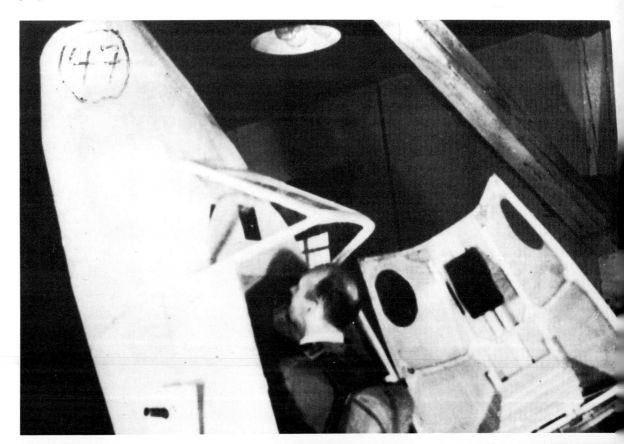

Right: Mock-up of the fuselage with rotatable pilot seat.

Top:
Final assembly of
the Bachem Ba
349. The engine
is recognisable in
the aircraft on the
left.

On 14 December 1944 was presumably the first towed flight of the BP 20 M3 in Neuburg/Donau which was followed on 22 December by a second. The take-off carriage for the M1 was located here as well. Due to bad weather conditions and the scarcity of tow aircraft, no further test flights were possible. In addition, there was a shortage of work space and billeting as well as workshops and transportation connections.

Meanwhile, it was felt necessary to attempt the first test of a vertical take-off using the launch gantry. This was to take place on the Heuberg near Stetten am kalten Markt. Propulsion was provided by the four solid fuel rockets which should lift the aircraft one second after ignition. This, however, is not what happened because the extinguishing equipment was melted by the heat of the rockets. During the ensuing heat build-up, the wooden "Natter" caught fire and burned itself out. Four days later a successful unmanned take-off attempt was made. At the same time, a successful launch was made by a BP 20 behind the He 111 H-6 (DG+RN) of the DFS. Due to personnel difficulties, flight activity was quiet for the next few weeks. A fire in the factory at Bodenbach stagnated the delivery of booster rockets to Heuberg, and the ensuing shortage delayed testing.

In the period of December 1944 to 31 January 1945, wind tunnel test with a scale model of the "Natter" were conducted by the DVL. In addition to various wing and tail configurations, different fuselage shapes and weapons configurations were studied.

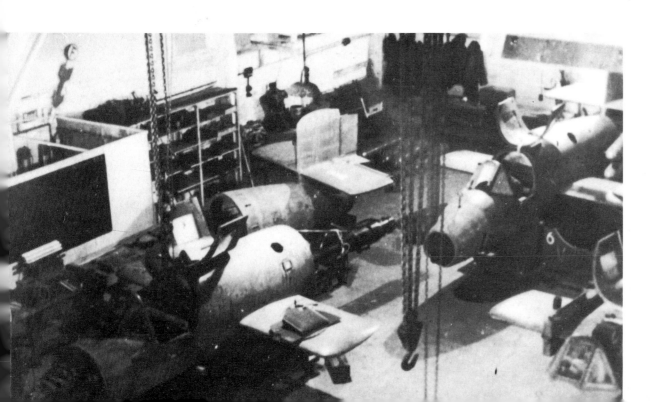

Bottom: The same scene from a different perspective. The rocket armament "Föhn" of the "Natter" is visible in the nose.

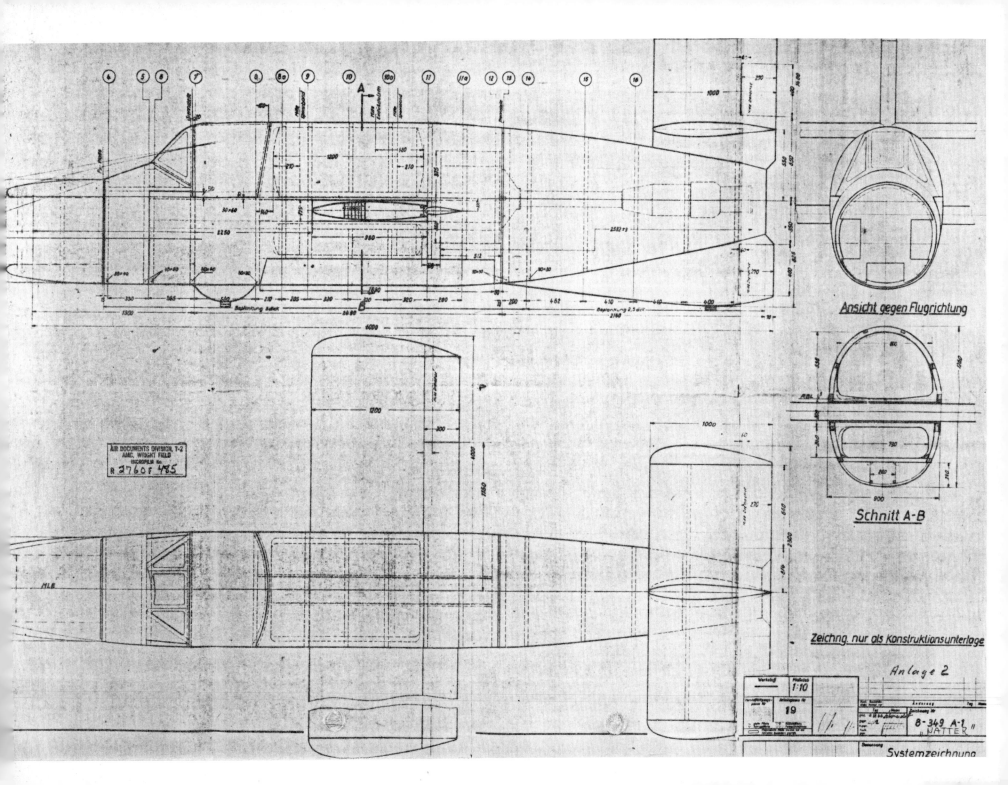

Ansicht gegen Flugrichtung

Schnitt A-B

Zeichng. nur als Konstruktionsunterlage

Anlage 2

Systemzeichnung

B-349 A-1 "NATTER"

Maßstab 1:10

Anlagen zu
19

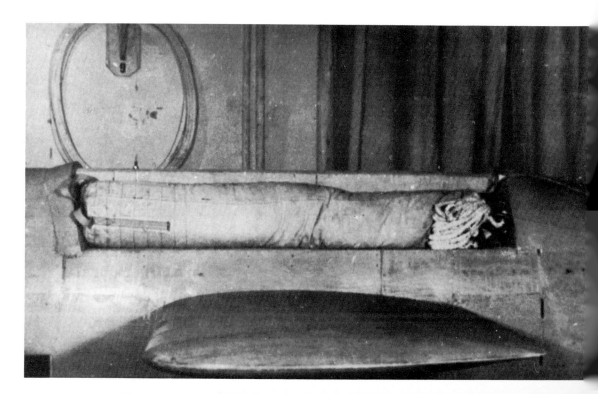

Above: In the unpowered prototype, the recovery parachute was located in the tail of the aircraft.

Right: Location of the recovery parachute in the production models of the "Natter" was on the top rear of the fuselage.

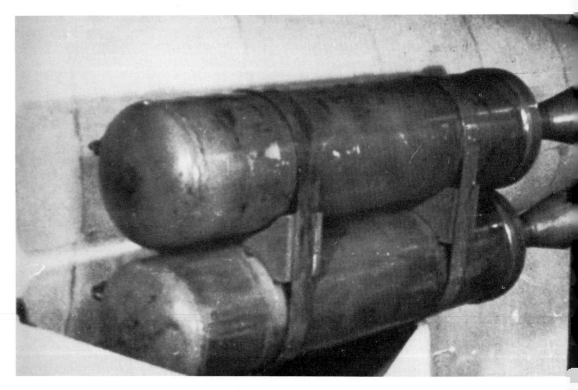

Placement of the four 500 kp booster rockets on a mock-up of
the BP-20.

Left: Sideview of a test version with two 100 kp. take-off assist rockets. Below: The aircraft was transported by carriage.

By the end of January 1945 the towing trials could finally begin again with Flugkaptän Zitter with the He 111 and the BP 20 M3.

In the ensuing weeks, the SS became more and more interested in the "Natter." Reichsführer Heinrich Himmler, let it be known that the Bachem "Natter" belonged to his department and its development was to be accelerated.

Positive results were obtained from the towed flights. It was now possible to undertake a free flight from a tow. This was first accomplished by Unteroffizer Hans Zübert on 14 February 1945 in the BP 20 M8.

On 25 Feb 1945, Heuberg was able to achieve the first full vertical take-off with proper equipment separation. The pilot mannequin as well as the empennage floated safely down on their parachutes. Earlier, a "Natter" burned up due to an explosion of the booster rockets on the gantry. Other machines spun so much that the tests accomplished little.

The success encouraged the SS main headquarters to attempt a manned vertical take-off of the "Natter." Lothar Sieber volunteered although he knew the immense risk involved.

On 01 March 1945 he entered the BP 20 M23 on the gantry. The prototype gained altitude quickly, pulled backwards to a 30 degree angle, completed a half roll, and disappeared seconds later into the clouds. Everything was going as planned. After approximately 50 seconds the "Natter" reappeared plummeting to earth. The pilot had become unconscious for an unexplained reason and had therefore not initiated the separation. He crashed together with the 23rd prototype in the vicinity of the gantry. The sole manned take-off attempt was ruined.

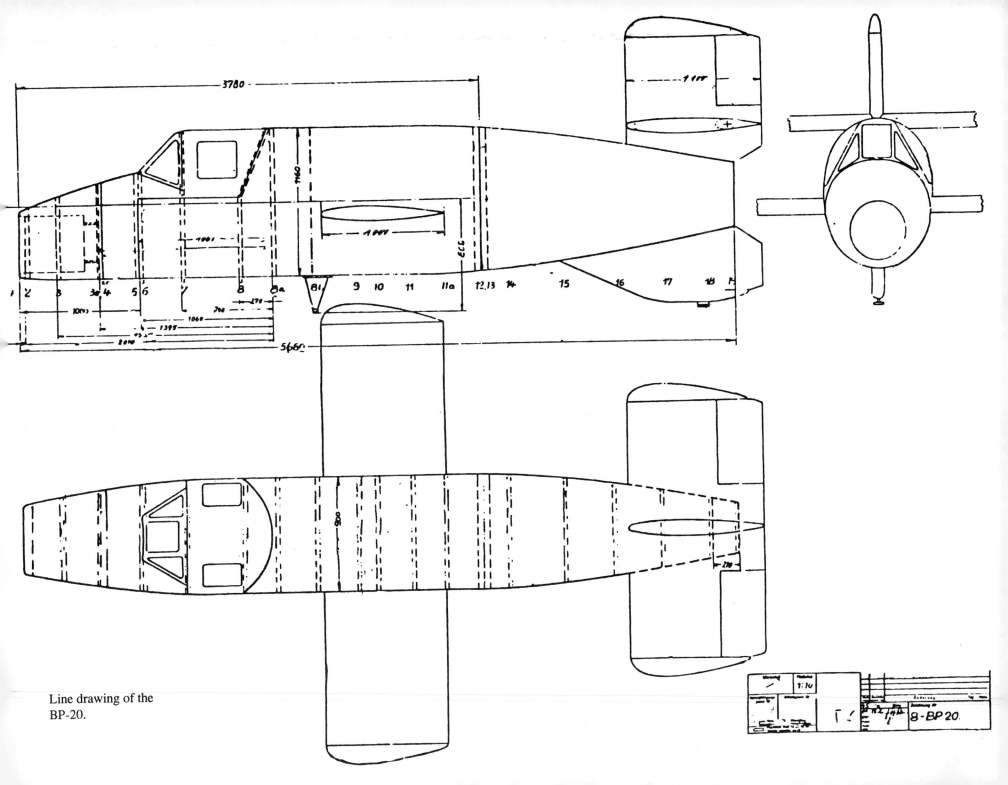

Line drawing of the
BP-20.

Despite the difficult personnel situation, it was possible to ready more prototypes by the end of March 1945. They included two unmanned, remote-controlled, powered aircraft, the M13 and 14 as well as the BP 20 M24 and 34. The M25, a prototype with stabilizers, and the M33 were also ready for use. Simultaneously, tests were done on a simplified 9m gantry. As a last resort, even telegraph poles were used as a take-off structure.

Engine and recovery testing were conducted at Heuberg with the BP 20 M22. The experiments were only partially successful. The same applied to the test aircraft M31 and M32.

Above left: Construction of one of the later towed prototypes. The tricycle style landing gear is already installed.

Left: Production of the "Natter" at the Bachem factory in Bad Waldsee.

Opposite page:
Above left: A BP-20 in tow under a He 111. The tow cable was installed in this instance on the upper wing. Certain cable motions which were a danger to pilots and machines could thus be minimized.

Below left: Completed prototype with landing gear for towing tests.

Above and below Right:
The BP-20 M8 served in February 1945 in towing tests.

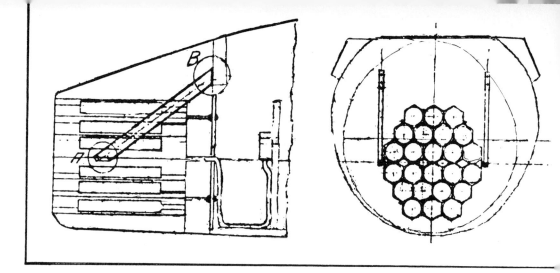

Above:
Detail of the installation plans for a variant of the "Föhn."

Above and right: Installation study for the rocket weapon "Föhn" in the nose of the BP-20. Because of its appearance, it was nicknamed the "rocket honeycomb" (Raketenwabe).

Right:
Installation plans for the rocket weapon "Grosse Rohrbatterie 108."

Below:
An unidentified variant for the Bachem "Natter" separated with the entire nose section from the fuselage.

Below Right:
Test stand assembly for live fire testing with the "Rohrbatterie 108." This was to replace the "Föhn" rocket launcher.

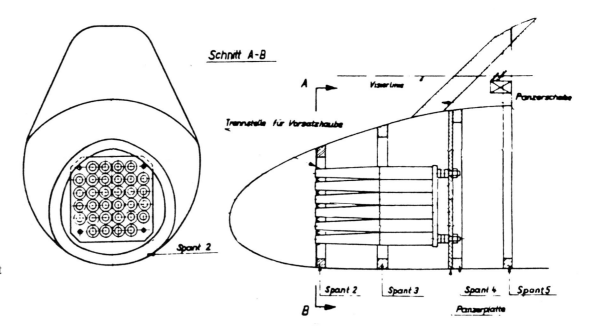

Schnitt A-B

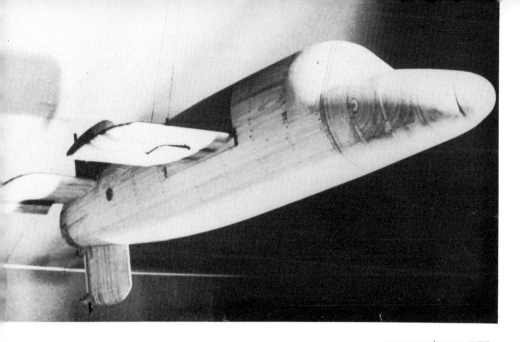

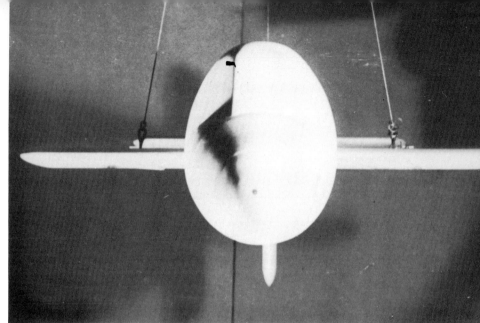

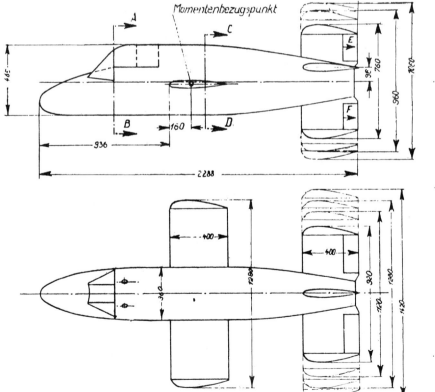

Momentenbezugspunkt

Schnitt A-B

Schnitt C-D

Schnitt E-F

Above left and above:
Wind tunnel models of the BP-20 used to measure various tail assemblies.

Left:
Overview drawing for wind tunnel testing of various tail assemblies by the DVL.

Opposite page:
An unmanned vertical take off of a BP-20 took place at the end of December 1944 at Heuberg. The photos clearly show the launch gantry and its construction.

Despite these problems, the technical requirements for the lifting mechanism and the initial operational use were solved in March 1945.

A portion of the project was move to Waldhausen although it possessed no available barracks and tools and equipment were kept outside. Vehicles to transport the "Natter" were not available in sufficient quantity. The intervention of the SS was not enough to supply transportation to deliver engines. Cement for concrete counterweights was not even available. During this time, the SS was developing plans for the operational use of the "N" machine. This was especially so after discussions that the Flak Section E5 might oversee the "Natter." Erich Bachem guarantied a deadline of 10 May 1945.

The operational use would go as follows: After an air raid warning, the ground crew would go to the machine and acquire the target. The pilot who had been sitting cockpit alert would switch on the on-board power. The orientation of the launch gantry would be constantly changed according to the latest information; i.e. the "Natter" would be generally oriented so it would meet the enemy formation. When the ready command was given, the ground crew were to clear the launch area and seek cover. The pilot set the engine and tested the flight controls. On the launch command the pilot was to press the start button and hold onto the hand grips with both hands. Everything else would be taken over by the automatic controls.

Fund bei Kommandantur
Truppenübungsplatz Heuberg
melden
Tel.Stetten am kalten Markt 222
Belohnung!

**Above:**
The painting of this unmanned powered machine helped control the flight from the ground.

**Above Left:**
A reconstruction of the machine in this picture stands today in the aircraft section of the German Museum in Munich.

**Left:**
Enlargement of the text on the empennage of the above mentioned reconstruction.

The BP-20 takes off with the help of booster rockets.

Right:
The BP-20 M22 during engine and parachute testing.

Below:
The BP-20 M33 only had booster rockets for propulsion. The Walter rocket system was not installed.

Opposite page:
Left: The "Natter" is set up with a tow cable. In the foreground are the pumps for fuelling.

Right: Fuelling the rocket fighter on the launch pad.

Below:
A powered machine is brought to the launch gantry. Left of center is a container (a milk can) for fuel (T-Stoff).

Only when in the immediate vicinity of the target would the pilot turn towards the enemy bombers and fire his 24 "Föhn" projectiles. Afterwards he would turn and at a safe distance release the recovery parachute.

Not only was it impossible in 1945 to construct the 20 "Natters" per month as ordered, there was not enough available fuel. The 520kg of fuel (T-Stoff) and 120kg of catalyst (C-Stoff) which were necessary for each flight could only be produced on paper because the required equipment for its production was not in operation before May 1945. This did not satisfy Himmler's order to produce sufficient specialty fuels.

On 20 March 1945 General Dornberger cancelled the Bachem Ba 349. The SS suddenly had no interest in the project as well. Nevertheless, in the beginning of April construction of the rocket fighter was resumed in Waldsee and Nabern unter Teck. A shortage of spare parts put the continued production into question.

After the middle of April 1945 preparations were made to transfer the Bachem works to Bad Wörrishofen. On 24 April 1945, French tank troops reached Waldsee. Ing. Zacher sank the last 15 remaining HWK engines in the nearby lake.

Because Bad Wörrishofen was only a temporary location, most of the workers, pilots with their five operational prototypes, vital construction documents, and sufficient spare parts were moved to St. Leonhard in Austria. Here during the beginning of May 1945, American soldiers captured them, four complete "Natters," a few solid-fuel rockets, spare parts, as well as other materials. Technical documents and plans were also of interest to the Americans.

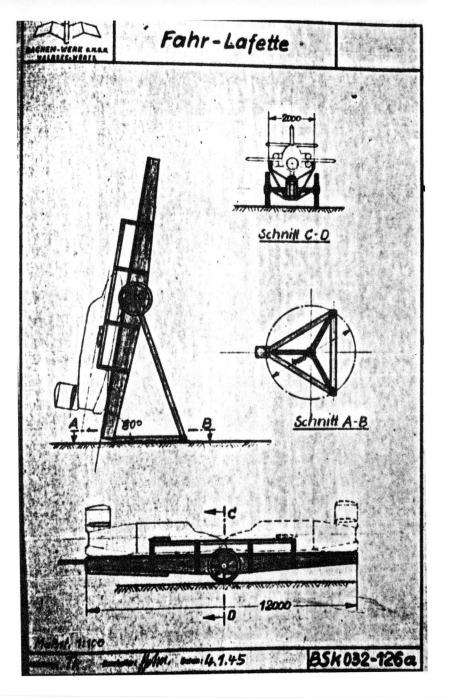

Fahr-Lafette

Schnitt C-D

Schnitt A-B

Opposite page:
Left: The Bachem Ba 349 is ready for take off. The marking on the wings were to help technical personnel monitor the flight profile, e.g. spinning on the longitudinal axis.

Center: Overview of a machine ready for take off. A pulley for erecting the machine is visible at the top.

Right: The gantry was simply a wooden pole (e.g. telegraph pole) which had guide rails attached to it. This was a way to avoid a permanent launch point and ensure a mobile system.

Above:
The first manned take off took place on 01 March 1945 in the BP-20 M23.

Above right:
This gantry was another idea for a mobile "Natter."

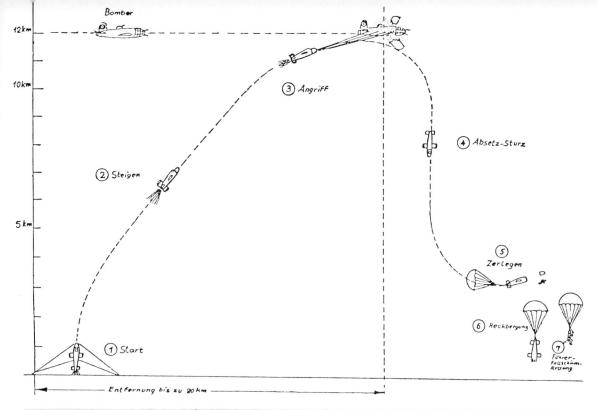

Left:
Planned operational profile of the Bachem Ba 349 "Natter." The drawing comes from the project description of the rocket fighter.

Below left:
Lothar Sieber, pictured in a flight suit, was the only one to take off vertically in the "Natter."

Below:
The pilot of the BP-20 M23 was killed in the test flight.

Drawing:
1. Take off          5. Ejection
2. Climb            6. Fuselage recovery
3. Attack           7. Pilot recovery
4. Landing dive

One of the Bachem Ba 349's found in St. Leonhard by the Americans.

In total, there were 30 Ba 349 "Natters" completed or in the final stage of assembly. Whether or not any others were under construction in Hirth is not clear.

At least one BP 20 fell into the hands of the Soviets. This machine was found in Thüringen where the Ba 349 was to be made under licence as fast as possible.

Lastly, it was hinted that at the end of 1944 the FAG Stettin concern under the direction of Ing. Göhring was building 1/2 scale models of the "Natter" which had solid fuel rockets in the rear fuselage. These were to used to study catapult launches. In this, the models were towed by three or four cables which pulled at the same speed. A take-off in February 1945 in Peenemünde was, however, a failure. The recirculation of the rocket gasses caused the recovery parachute to deploy and the model "Natter" was pulled off course. The course of the war prevented further testing.

Interior view of the nose. Left are the control pedals, right under the armored glass.

The Bachem "Natter" found by the Americans in St. Leonard was equipped with "Föhn" rockets.

# Technical Data
## of the project "Natter (BP-20/Barak I) according to the description of 27 November 1944

## Performance

| | |
|---|---|
| Maximum altitude | 16,000 m |
| Speed during climb | 675 km/h |
| Acceleration at take off | 2.2 g |
| Vertical speed of | 675 km/h |
| attained in | 1,000 m |
| Max vertical speed at 5,000 m | 1,000 km/h |

| | | |
|---|---|---|
| Normal speed | | 800 km/h |
| Endurance | ca | 7 min |
| Range at 12,000 m | | |
| 1. With boosters, engines set at 100 kp thrust | | 80 km |
| 2. Without boosters, engines set at 300 kp thrust | | 41 km |
| 3. Additional glide range in horizontal flight. | | 14 km |

## Dimensions

| | |
|---|---|
| Length | 6.02 m |
| Wing span | 4.00 m |
| Height without undercarriage | 1.30 m |
| Fuselage width | 0.90 m |
| Height with undercarriage | 2.23 m |
| Wing width | 1.20 m |
| Wing loading, full | 568 kg/sq m |
| Wing loading, empty | 233 kg/sq m |

## Weight

| | |
|---|---|
| Rudder | 25 kg |
| Flight controls | 35 kg |
| Pilot and gear | 100 kg |
| Pilot seat | 4 kg |
| Aircraft nosecone | 17 kg |
| Weapons and ammunition | 185 kg |
| Armored glass | 25 kg |
| Instrumentation | 6 kg |
| Armor plating | 139 kg |
| Accumulator | 25 kg |
| Fuselage center section and wings | 117 kg |
| Fuel tanks and 750 kg fuel | 793 kg |
| Engine | 170 kg |
| 2 Recovery parachutes | 80 kg |
| Rear fuselage | 30 kg |
| Stabilizers | 59 kg |
| 4 Booster rockets delivering 1200kp thrust with 10s burn time @ 115kg each | 460 kg |
| Total | 2270 kg |

Fully armed operational machines were found amongst the machines captured at St. Leonhard.

## Bachem NATTER

| | | | |
|---|---|---|---|
| BP 20 | M 1 | Towed flights behind He 111 H-6 (DG+RN) in Neuburg. First towed flight on 22 Dec 1944. |
| BP 20 | M 2 | Test flown with Kl 35 - Tricycle landing gear |
| BP 20 | M 3 | Towing test like BP 20 M1, afterwards rebuilt. First towed flight on 14 Dec 1944. |
| BP 20 | M 4 | Planned for towing/separation trials. |
| BP 20 | M 5 | Planned for towing/separation trials. |
| BP 20 | M 6 | Planned for towing/separation trials. |
| BP 20 | M 7 | Planned for towing/separation trials. |
| BP 20 | M 8 | Completed with brace for piggy-back launch. Successful separation in flight on 9 February 1945. |
| BP 20 | M 9 | Prototype under construction in Waldsee during January 1945. |
| BP 20 | M 10 | Planned for towing/separation trials. |
| BP 20 | M 11 | Planned for unmanned vertical launch. |
| BP 20 | M 12 | Planned for unmanned vertical launch. |
| BP 20 | M 13 | Unmanned rocket aircraft with remote controls. |
| BP 20 | M 14 | Unmanned rocket aircraft with remote controls. |
| BP 20 | M 15 | Unmanned rocket aircraft with remote controls. |
| BP 20 | M 16 | Launched from 17m gantry with remote controls. |
| BP 20 | M 17 | Launched from 12.5m gantry to 2500m altitude. |
| BP 20 | M 18 | Unmanned rocket test aircraft. |
| BP 20 | M 19 | Unmanned rocket test aircraft. |
| BP 20 | M 20 | Unmanned rocket test aircraft. |
| BP 20 | M 21 | Unmanned rocket test aircraft. |
| BP 20 | M 22 | Vertical launch, engine, and parachute test aircraft. |
| BP 20 | M 23 | Manned launch on 1 March 1945 with all equipment. |
| BP 20 | M 24 | Unmanned machine under construction on 1 March 1945. |
| BP 20 | M 25 | Manned machine under construction on 1 March 1945. |
| BP 20 | M 26 | Disposition unknown. |
| BP 20 | M 27 | Disposition unknown. |
| BP 20 | M 28 | Disposition unknown. |
| BP 20 | M 29 | Disposition unknown. |
| BP 20 | M 30 | Disposition unknown. |
| BP 20 | M 31 | Launch from 8m gantry for parachute testing. |
| BP 20 | M 32 | Launch for gantry testing. |
| BP 20 | M 33 | Unmanned launch. |
| BP 20 | M 34 | Manned rocket aircraft under construction on 1 March 1945. |
| Ba 349 A | | First production aircraft under construction on 1 March 1945. |
| Ba 349 B | | Rebuilt aircraft from the Waldsee production. |
| Ba 349 C | | Series production with improved wings. |

The aircraft were captured intact. Undamaged plans, equipment and spare parts also fell into the American's hands.

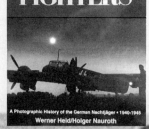